Poems for my ex

Cici Han

ISBN 978-93-5610-086-2

Published in India 2022 by Pencil

A brand of
One Point Six Technologies Pvt. Ltd.
123, Building J2, Shram Seva Premises,
Wadala Truck Terminal, Wadala (E)
Mumbai 400037, Maharashtra, INDIA
E connect@thepencilapp.com
W www.thepencilapp.com

Author biography

Cici Han is a twenty one year budding writer pursuing Masters in Counseling. She considers writing her therapy because of which this book has come into existence. Writing this book is a small part of her healing process from her recent failed relationship. She's optimistic, vibrant, kind and goal driven.

CONTENTS

Preface

The book has been divided into two sections: Part 1 & 2. It wasn't meant to be this way but here we are.

Part 1 comprises of seven poems I wrote a few days before my break up and Part 2 includes poems I've written for the same person post-break up. I hope you experience all the different emotions that I felt when I wrote the poems. Thankyou for reading.

Acknowledgements

Dear C,

Even in deep sorrow, I love you

Part 1

Seventh

For the only person I've ever loved,
I'm his seventh.
Seven isn't such a bad number
But not good enough for me to be not envious
Envious of all those who came before me
Who received his love, his kisses and his hugs
I'm envious of the times he was there for them when they needed them
I'm envious of the times they held his hand and kissed him
I'm envious of the time I couldn't spend with him
I'm envious of the time he couldn't spend with me
But I'm grateful to be his seventh
He went through six types of hurt
Six types he doesn't inflict on me
He protects me six times more
He loves me harder than he has ever loved those six beautiful women
He hugs me and kisses me in ways that tell me that I'm his last.
I'm grateful to those six beautiful women who made him happy in six different ways,
Now I make him happy in a hundred ways and counting
I'm his seventh and I'm his last.

Every Thought

I tried to pen down my thoughts
I realized you're all of my thoughts
You occupy every part of my brain,
Every chamber of my heart
You are all of my thoughts and all my thoughts have you in it
It has been since the day I told you I liked you
I lied that day
I told you I liked you when I was neck deep in love.
You occupy every single part of my thoughts.
I love you.

This Christmas

This Christmas I'm full

I don't need any presents

My delivery came one year early

It covers all the Christmases I'll celebrate til I die

My present is like no other

He breathes, eats and sleeps

He does other things too

My present is kind, beautiful

He makes me happy like no other

My present is the one I think of all day

The ones who reciprocates the same

This Christmas I am full

He is my present for a second time

And I don't need anything else

The moon & Him

The moon was up alone
The stars left her, so did the clouds
Nobody cared to look at her long enough
She longed for company
Company which no one wanted to give her
She was broken and she began to fade more each passing night
"No body will ever notice even if I just leave"
She thought as she faded away completely into the pitch black sky.

He was walking home again
His phone in his hand
No notifications
No calls
He had given his heart to someone
Not sure if that someone had kept it or thrown it
He looked up the sky looking for his friend 'the moon, the beauty'
The sky was pitch black
Lonely like himself
His only friend was the moon
He would talk to the moon each night while he waited for his phone to ring
"Even the moon has left me" He said
As he walked home.

My sun

Where are you, my sun?

My body is longing for warmth that radiates from you

The clouds have taken over the sky and the cold air is biting my skin

My body has shrunk into a ball of desperation

I'm cold and I'm tired of the walls echoing my long sad breaths

Where are you, my sun?

My eyes are dimmed with the loneliness of the clouds

My heart is restless and my soul is angered

Your presence makes a difference my dear sun.

Your beauty

Brown beautiful eyes,
Your brown beautiful eyes.
I can't ever have enough of those brown beautiful eyes.
Everytime you gaze at me I trespass inside
I see great beauty and love and comfort
I wish I could see myself from your eyes
Because from your eyes I am so much better, I am so much more attractive
Those eyes, those brown beautiful eyes
Why can't we have the same view?
Your eyes see beauty in places I see nothing
Your eyes are blind to the places I often acknowledge, the dark & ugly nooks and corners
How can you look over such?
How can you only see beauty?
Sigh it is you who is beautiful but not me
It is your beauty you see in me
It is your beauty that glows from within that you reflect on me
How can you not see anything but beauty when you are so beautiful yourself!

You are my sun

This morning it was foggy and cold

It reminded me of myself when you once left me all alone

The air was dry and bitter

Like how our conversations were when you stopped texting me like you used to

I can't deny that I miss you most on days like today

When the body is cold and the heart too

The sun out shined the fog at noon, like the time you kissed me even after we broke up

You couldn't stay away from me

Neither can I stay away from you

The sun reminded me of our reconciliation and your love that provides me the warmth that I need on days like today

I've said it before

And I'll say it again

You're my sun.

Part 2

You led me

You led me on to believe that your love was real and you journeyed away,

I smiled as you left and prayed for your safe journey because I knew you'd come back for me.

I knew nothing!

You returned a changed man,

You fell in love immediately with some one else.

How is that even possible?

You told me you were busy,

I believed you.

I smiled imagining you talking to your grandfather sipping a cup of bitter black tea,

Warming your body near the fire that shone brightly

I hoped it would remind you of my love for you.

But you moved on to someone else,

You didn't even tell me.

As I prayed every night for your safety,

You were safely holding her in your arms.

Kissing her and protecting her with your best security.

You led me on to believe you were actually guilty

I believed you

I forgave you.

24 hours

Within the 24 hours you confessed that you cheated shattering my hopes completely

I shed a tear or two and I forgave you

I believed it was a mistake

I believed that you were too good to do that

You hurt me but I was guilty

I loved you too much to imagine you being choked by the vines of guilt

I loved you that much.

You hurt me but I still prayed for you

I still hoped that you'd love me back and we'd go back to the times we smiled together.

Little did I know that you took my smile to give it to her.

12 months

One year of giving my all to you

You accepted everything with love like you claimed

Gone is the year and now it's time for someone new to give you her everything

You said I'll be your last

Why did I believe you?

I told you, 'You're the only one I love' and that was absolutely true

You didn't warn me about you changing and falling out of love so soon

You didn't tell me that your love came with a limit

You bartered your 12 months with my entire lifetime

Gone are the 12 months and so are you.

I wish you'd have warned me before I fell into the pitch black pit of love,

what now seems to be only unrequited.

Write for you

I told you I'd write you a book to pen down my endless love for you

You smiled and waited patiently

Your patience is now over

And your love is now gone

Mine however remains but it is contaminated with the betrayal and ache you freely gave me as you parted from me while I was awaiting your return

I'll keep my end of the bargain and I'll write you a book

You'll still be my muse but the words will not be of the love that was pure I had for you

Everything I pen down for write what I have left of you,

Know that it is filled with love of the dejected kind, and ache, that I hope you'll feel if you ever read this.

My skin

They say that the skin remembers maybe that's why it hurts so much

It still reeks of the smell of yours

It still longs for the touch

But you betrayed my skin

yours no longer smells like mine anymore

They say that the skin remembers

Maybe thats why I cry at night when I feel my hands running down your stubby beard and pink chapped lips

Lips now invaded by another,

Your stubby beard now piercing someone else's skin.

They say that the skin remembers,

Maybe that's why I hate you even more.

My skin can never not love you

My skin will never forget

My senses will never be the same

And You're the only one to blame.

Displaced

How am I supposed to make you experience the displacement you've made me feel as I slip under the warmth of my blanket,
my heart aches for time that has passed long ago
The time that will not return
Even if it does it won't be the same.

Hard to breathe

When I confessed that I love you,

I found it hard to breathe

I'd never been so in touch with that part of my brain that it felt alien to my body.

When I started loving you I told you without you I find it hard to breathe,

You laughed it off.

You thought I was being childish and faking it

Maybe you didn't believe me because you didn't love me as hard as I did.

Now that you are gone, I find it harder to breathe.

I take long breaths yet I don't feel the oxygen in my lungs

My tears fall

My chest tightens

You'd still not believe me if I told you

But I don't find the need to prove

My love over and over again

My actions were louder than me gasping for air yet it wasn't enough to make you stay

Maybe I've always meant it when I said I love you more.

12:12 AM

It's 12:12 AM and I wonder if you're sleeping

You didn't ask but I can't sleep

You left but you still occupy every part of my brain (and heart)

Thoughts of you keep me awake through out the night

They haunt me all day long

You left me but you didn't take our memories with you

I'm hurting alone

You found someone you plan on sharing your life with

It makes me feel lonelier you know

I have no one to tell how my day was spent,

I have no one to share my hurt

You were my safe person

You were the one

But you turned your back in me in moments I needed you the most

I waited and you did turn to face me again

But you faced me to bid farewell

What am I to do with this heart I cannot carry?

It's too heavy for me to go on

This weight had blinded me

My life's purpose is blurred

Why did you leave me like this?

You shouldn't have entered my life if you were going to leave like this.

I can't go on but I have to

It's so difficult for me

I wish to stop breathing

But you'd not even bother to see if I'm still alive.

Every night

Every night I go to bed

Thinking of the love we once had

I cannot keep them off my mind

I wonder how is it so easy for you?

Do you not think of the time we first met after dating?

My shy smile meeting your nervous one

I couldn't stop looking at you, I thought you were so beautiful that it made my chest ache in happiness of course

I'm crying as I write this because I still think you're beautiful

When your hands first touched mine and the butterflies in my stomach couldn't stop giving me the tickles

Your hands were home to mine

It just felt right sitting next to you.

Mother left the room and in a millisecond you kissed my cheek and my wheatish skin turned pink and hot.

You took the next step and stole a kiss, I smiled cause it was special.

You are my first kiss, I wish I was yours too.

When we ate our lunch, I couldn't stop staring at how cute you looked when you were devouring the food mother made for you,

I was full without eating because seeing you happy was satisfying enough.

I think of the many other good times I had with you,

Tears can't help but trickle down my face because you've replaced me with her to make better memories with.

Don't you ever think of our good times?

Don't you ever smile thinking of me? Or are you so busy looking at the beauty you've bagged that you've stopped dwelling on the nightmares from your past?

You love your space

You told me you need space

You broke my heart

But it isn't the first time so I can handle that

Maybe after a while you'll love me again like you always do

Well I guess I was so used to you not needing me that it hurt me less when you said that.

You told me you kissed someone else and I cried because I couldn't believe you resting your lips on someone else's

You promised me you'd never lay your eyes on someone who isn't me

You'd never wish to kiss anybody other than me

What happened to those promises?

I believe that it was a mistake and I forgave you because I didn't want to lose you.

I missed you and I prayed you'd miss me too.

I dreamt that you moved on and you did move on

You confessed and I cried

I still loved you

How could you move on so easily?

What happened to the love you professed to me?

Was it a lie or was your love too weak to be loyal to me?

You said you've decided to love her

The most painful sentence I've been told

So casually like I didn't matter at all.

My once in a life time

I believe love comes once in a lifetime

You are my love

You are my once in a lifetime

I gave you everything I had and everything I thought you needed

I loved you like no other.

But I'm not the love you want to be with for a lifetime

Now that's too painful to bear

What am I to do with the plans we made together?

You made it seem like you had our future figured out

Left with nothing

I don't think I have ever seen anybody quite as heartless as you

You made me feel whole when you were actually deconstructing me to pieces

By the time I saw your changed self

Nothing of me was left to give me solace

You took everything

Now I'm left with nothing.

My soul knew

My soul knew that you were doing more than what you made me believe,

My heart had no clue.

My soul cried for weeks,

My heart had to bear the pain without understanding the reason why.

My heart blamed my mind for going to places it shouldn't,

My mind couldn't help but continue to do so.

My soul cried a river and it flowed from Christmas Eve til the New year without knowing the origin and the destination.

My heart had no clue

My mind was busy

My soul linked to yours when we consummated knew that you had touched someone else

My soul knew that your arms were resting on hands which didn't belong to me

My soul knew you were caressing a body which is not mine

Your soul linked to mine

And mine linked to yours

Yet you managed to loosen the tie enough to break my soul

My soul knew

My heart didn't

My soul knew.

The river and I

Tonight I escaped the crowd and went to the Riverside

Quiet, Cold & foggy

Just like the state of my heart

I like to believe that you loved me atleast for a short while,

How I wish it lasted longer.

My love is like the river before me,

It was so full of love during summer when you rained your love on me and I collected it and it flowed through beautifully.

It's winter now and you've stopped showering me with love.

The water before me may seem shallow

The river bed may be visible in some places

But don't you see there's still water?

That's my love for you

Even if you don't give me your love

The love you have given me before sustains me

The riverbed that I can see from where I'm sitting is the hurt you've caused me by being frugal with your love.

An open wound surfacing,

Visible enough for the world to know what's missing.

The fog and the chill air surrounds me bringing me more pain to my open wounds, if you're with me I won't be in the cold. I'll be in the warmth of your embrace.

But you've moved on and

I am here gazing at the distant lights across the river hoping that they give me the solace you give me no more.

www.ingramcontent.com/pod-product-compliance
Lightning Source LLC
LaVergne TN
LVHW040726170726
843469LV00079B/1282

9789356100862